CHILDREN'S AND PARENTS' SERVICES
PATCHOGUE-MEDFORD LIBRARY

Fact Finders™

Land and Water

The Yangtze River

by Nathan Olson

Consultant:
Robert M. Hordon, Ph.D., P.H.
Department of Geography
Rutgers University
Piscataway, New Jersey

Capstone
press
Mankato, Minnesota

The Yangtze

In western China, water begins a great journey. It melts from a sheet of ice. The water rushes over waterfalls and races around sharp curves. It smashes against rocks. It speeds up, and **rapids** begin to form. The rapids toss and turn, shooting the water through narrow mountain paths.

The water then slows into a calm river. It flows past green cliffs and large cities. Boats on the river move people and goods. Farmers use the river water to grow rice. Fishers catch salmon in the river. The water of the Yangtze River ends its journey when it flows into the East China Sea.

The Yangtze

In western China, water begins a great journey. It melts from a sheet of ice. The water rushes over waterfalls and races around sharp curves. It smashes against rocks. It speeds up, and **rapids** begin to form. The rapids toss and turn, shooting the water through narrow mountain paths.

The water then slows into a calm river. It flows past green cliffs and large cities. Boats on the river move people and goods. Farmers use the river water to grow rice. Fishers catch salmon in the river. The water of the Yangtze River ends its journey when it flows into the East China Sea.

Table of Contents

Fact Finders is published by Capstone Press
151 Good Counsel Drive, P.O. Box 669, Mankato, Minnesota 56002
www.capstonepress.com

Copyright © 2004 by Capstone Press. All rights reserved.
No part of this publication may be reproduced in whole or in part, or stored in a retrieval
system, or transmitted in any form or by any means, electronic, mechanical, photocopying,
recording, or otherwise, without written permission of the publisher.
For information regarding permission, write to Capstone Press,
151 Good Counsel Drive, P.O. Box 669, Dept. R, Mankato, Minnesota 56002.
Printed in the United States of America

Library of Congress Cataloging-in-Publication Data
Olson, Nathan.
    The Yangtze River / by Nathan Olson.
    p. cm.—(Fact finders. Land and water)
    Includes bibliographical references and index.
    Contents: The Yangtze—The Yangtze's path—The Yangtze's history—The Yangtze's
people—Using the Yangtze—The Yangtze today.
    ISBN 0-7368-2485-5 (hardcover)
    1. Yangtze River (China)—Juvenile literature. [1. Yangtze River (China)] I. Title.
II. Series.
DS793.Y3O46 2004
915.1'2—dc22   2003013986

Editorial Credits
Erika L. Shores, editor; Juliette Peters, series designer; Linda Clavel, book designer and
    illustrator; Alta Schaffer, photo researcher; Eric Kudalis, product planning editor

Photo Credits
Betty Crowell, 1, 16–17, 22
Corbis/AFP, 11; Keren Su, 7, 18–19; Liu Liqun, cover, 26–27; Yang Liu, 10
Corbis Sygma/Langevin Jacques, 23
Getty Images Inc./AFP, 24–25; AFP/Stephen Shaver, 4–5; Carl Mydans/Time Life Pictures,
    14; Dmitri Kessel/Time Life Pictures; 15
North Wind Picture Archives, 12–13
TRIP/H&J Blackwell, 20–21

Artistic Effects
Image Ideas Inc.

1 2 3 4 5 6 09 08 07 06 05 04

Fact Finders™

Land and Water

The Yangtze River

by Nathan Olson

Consultant:
Robert M. Hordon, Ph.D., P.H.
Department of Geography
Rutgers University
Piscataway, New Jersey

Capstone press
Mankato, Minnesota

Boats on the Yangtze River travel past huge cliffs.

The River

The Yangtze River flows 3,900 miles (6,300 kilometers) through China. The Yangtze is the third longest river in the world. Only the Nile River in Africa and the Amazon River in South America are longer.

Most Chinese call the river *Chang Jiang*. This name means long river or great river. Other people call the river *Jinsha Jiang*. It means the river of golden sand.

The Yangtze River is the third longest river in the world.

Chapter 2

The Yangtze's Path

The Yangtze River begins as tiny streams in the Tanggula Mountains of western China. The water flows south through **canyons** in the mountains. The fast water and deep canyons make the the river hard to use. Few people live in this area.

Three Gorges

The Yangtze flows north and then east into a series of **gorges**. Gorges are deep valleys with steep, rocky sides. The most famous part of the Yangtze is called Three Gorges. These gorges are called Qutang, Wuxia, and Xiling.

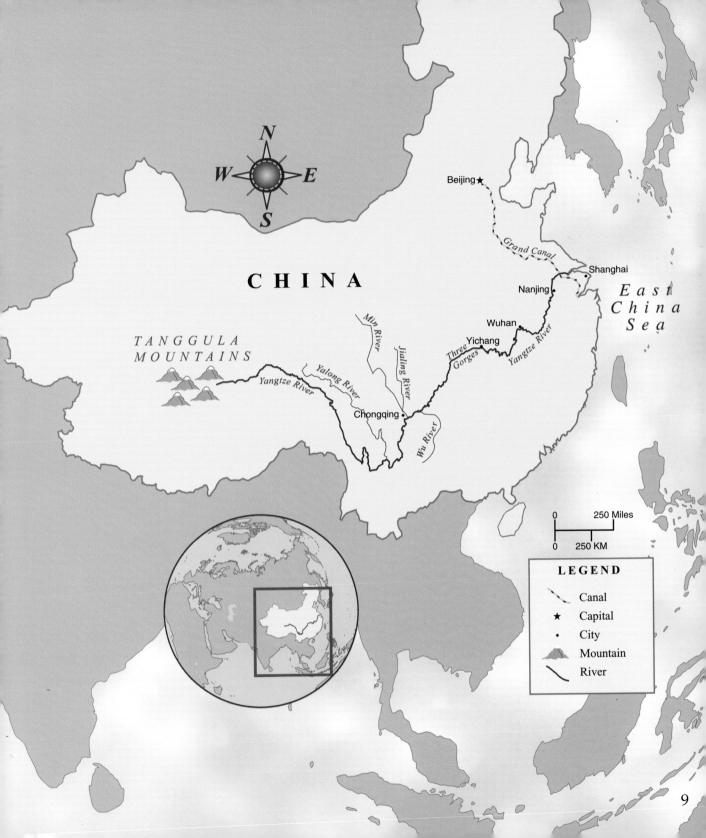

N
W E
S

Beijing ★

Grand Canal

Shanghai

CHINA

Nanjing

East China Sea

Wuhan

Min River

Jialing River

Yangtze River

Yichang

Three Gorges

TANGGULA MOUNTAINS

Yalong River

Yangtze River

Chongqing

Wu River

0   250 Miles
0   250 KM

LEGEND

〰 Canal
★ Capital
• City
⛰ Mountain
〰 River

Fast water rushes through the gorges' narrow openings and over rocks to make rapids. Rapids make the Three Gorges area dangerous for people and boats.

Into the Sea

Beyond the Three Gorges, the Yangtze flows through low, flat land. The river slows down. People use this part of the river for shipping, farming, and fishing. The river ends as it flows past the city of Shanghai and into the East China Sea.

▲ The Yangtze flows past Shanghai as it enters the East China Sea.

Monsoons

Rain is both important and dangerous to areas along the Yangtze. Strong winds, called **monsoons**, occur in spring and summer. They bring heavy rains to the area.

Monsoons add water to the river and keep it from drying up. Without monsoons, people would not have enough water to drink or to grow crops. Too much rainfall can flood the river. Many people have died when the Yangtze has flooded.

FACT!

From 1876 to 1879, monsoons did not occur. Many Chinese did not have enough water to grow crops. Between 9 and 13 million people starved to death.

Heavy rainfall brought by monsoons can cause the ▼ Yangtze to flood.

11

Chapter 3

The Yangtze's History

People have used the Yangtze for about 9,000 years. Farmers first settled near the river. They grew rice to eat and to feed their animals. Villages soon formed. Farmers worked and traded with each other.

China

People from northern China wanted to have the farmland near the river. They attacked and took over many villages along the Yangtze. They made the villages into states. These states fought each other for hundreds of years. Eventually, the states joined together and became the empire of China in 221 B.C.

Long ago, people used buckets to bring water from the Yangtze to their crops.

The rulers of China soon owned most of the land along the river. Peasants worked the land for the rulers. In return for living on the land, the peasants paid rulers with crops and labor. They built palaces for the rulers and cleared farmland.

▲ Boats travel on the Grand Canal from the Yangtze to Beijing.

F A C T !

The Grand Canal joins the city of Beijing with the Yangtze. The canal is about 1,119 miles (1,801 kilometers). It is the longest canal in the world.

Canals

The rulers also made peasants dig **canals**. Canals joined other rivers and lakes with the Yangtze. Boats then could take goods to and from other areas in China.

▲ Small boats called junks move people and goods on the Yangtze.

Boats picked up and dropped off goods where canals met the Yangtze. People began settling in these areas to earn money. Many of these areas became large cities. Today, many of China's largest cities lie along the Yangtze.

Chapter 4

The Yangtze's People

The Yangtze shows visitors both old and new China. The river flows through small villages and large, modern cities.

Village Life

The western half of the river shows the simple lives of Chinese farmers. Farmers live in small villages just as people did long ago. People use animals instead of machines to plow the earth. Their homes have no plumbing or electricity. People living along the Yangtze fish in the river. They also travel by boats on the river.

Farmers living in villages along the
Yangtze use animals to pull plows.

Modern China

As the Yangtze flows east, it moves through areas of modern China. Areas such as the Sichuan Basin are home to many people. The city of Chongqing has about 3 million people. It is one of China's largest cities.

The city of Shanghai is located where the Yangtze meets the sea. More than 9 million people live in Shanghai. It is a busy **port** city. Goods made in China are shipped from the port to other countries.

Boats travel up the Yangtze to bring people and goods to Chongqing, China.

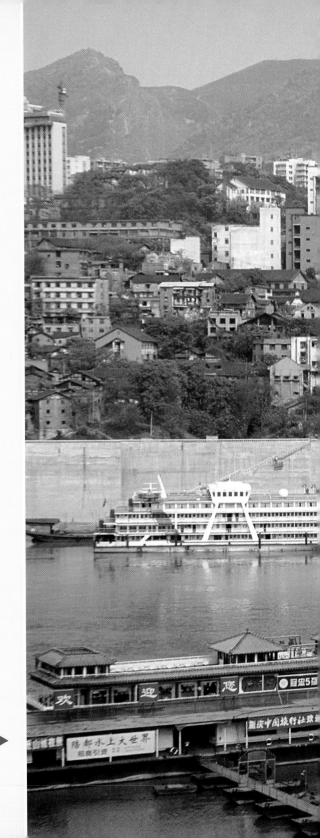

18

Chapter 5

Using the Yangtze

The Yangtze is still important to farming and other **industries**. Farmers use the land near the river to grow rice and raise pigs. They also grow cotton and wheat.

The last 500 miles (800 kilometers) of the Yangtze are some of the best fishing and farming areas in China. Farmers can grow crops there all year. The Chinese call this area "The Land of Fish and Rice."

The Chinese have built many factories along the Yangtze. Some of the factories process iron and steel. Iron and steel are used to make buildings and boats.

The land near the Yangtze is good for growing rice.

Hydroelectricity

The Chinese also have built **dams** on the Yangtze. Dams hold the river water back. People run water through a machine in the dam to make electricity. This type of electricity is called **hydroelectricity**. Hydro means water. The large amount of water in the Yangtze is a good source of hydroelectricity.

The Gezhouba Dam on the Yangtze is located ▼ near Yichang.

Environment

People using the Yangtze has damaged the **environment**. Factories sometimes dump chemicals into the river. The chemicals can kill fish and other water animals.

Farmers cut down trees to make more farmland. Fewer trees along the river cause loose soil to wash into the river when it rains. More soil in the river can cause flooding. The Chinese government is looking for ways to use the river without harming the environment.

▲ In some areas, pollution enters the Yangtze from open drain pipes.

F A C T !

Some animals that live in the Yangtze are dying out. About 100 Chinese River dolphins, or *baiji*, still live in the Yangtze. Boat traffic and pollution damages the areas where the *baiji* live.

Chapter 6

The Yangtze Today

Today, the Chinese are trying to make better use of the Yangtze. In 1993, the Chinese started building a dam in the Three Gorges area. The dam will be finished in 2009. It will be the largest dam in the world. The dam will give electricity and drinking water to many homes in China. The dam also may help control floods along the Yangtze.

Problems

Many people worry that the dam may make problems worse. A huge lake is forming behind the dam. To make room for the lake, at least 1 million people will lose their homes and farms.

People fish in the lake formed by the Three Gorges Dam.

Some people worry the dam could break and cause a huge flood. Others worry that building the dam will destroy the areas where rare plants and animals live.

Tourism

Many visitors come to the Yangtze each year. Tourists enjoy going on boat trips on the Yangtze. Tourists can see a large area of China in a short time.

FACT!

The power plant at Three Gorges will be the largest in the world.

The Yangtze is the most important river in China. For thousands of years, people have used the river for water, food, and trade. It is still used for those things today. The river even creates electricity for homes and businesses. In the years ahead, this useful river will continue to be important to the people of China.

Cruise ships take visitors up and down the Yangtze River. ◄

Fast Facts ━━━━

Source: streams in the Tanggula Mountains

Outlet: East China Sea

Name: In China, the name of the Yangtze is *Chang Jiang*. It means long river or great river. The Yangtze is also called *Jinsha Jiang*. It means river of golden sand.

Major tributaries: Yalong River, Min River, Jialing River, Wu River

Major industries: fishing, farming, shipping

Major cities: Shanghai, Wuhan, Chongqing, Nanjing

Hands On: Dig a Canal

Canals join lakes and other rivers with the Yangtze. Hundreds of years ago, Chinese people used hand shovels to dig canals. Their work made it easier for ships to travel across China. Try this activity and make your own canal.

What You Need

plastic spoon
a large plastic tub filled with tightly packed dirt
ruler
water

What You Do

1. Use the spoon to dig a hole about 6 inches (15 centimeters) across and about 3 inches (8 centimeters) deep in the dirt.
2. About 8 inches (20 centimeters) away, dig another hole about the same size as the first.
3. Fill the two holes with water.
4. Find a space about halfway between the two holes. Begin digging a narrow trench from this spot to one of the holes. Stop digging the trench about 1 inch (2.5 centimeters) before reaching the hole.
5. Go back to the halfway point and begin digging a narrow trench toward the other hole. Dig this trench all the way so it connects to that hole.
6. Now, join the trench to the first hole.
7. Does water flow into the trench? You have made a canal to join the two holes.

Many canals join lakes and rivers to the Yangtze. How would people travel from one river to another without the canals? How would people move goods without canals?

Glossary

canal (kun-NAL)—a channel that is dug across land; canals join bodies of water so that ships can travel between them.

canyon (KAN-yuhn)—a deep, narrow river valley with steep sides

dam (DAM)—a strong wall built across a stream or river to hold water back

environment (en-VYE-ruhn-muhnt)—the natural world of the land, water, and air

gorge (GORJ)—a deep valley with steep, rocky sides

hydroelectricity (hye-droh-e-lek-TRISS-uh-tee)—a form of energy caused by flowing water

industry (IN-duh-stree)—businesses that make products or provide services

monsoon (mon-SOON)—a very strong wind that blows across the Indian Ocean and southern Asia; in the summer, monsoons blow from the ocean toward land, bringing heavy rains.

port (PORT)—a place where boats and ships can dock safely

rapids (RAP-idz)—a place in a river where fast-moving water flows over rocks

Internet Sites

FactHound offers a safe, fun way to find Internet sites related to this book. All of the sites on FactHound have been researched by our staff.

Here's how:
1. Visit *www.facthound.com*
2. Type in this special code **0736824855** for age-appropriate sites. Or enter a search word related to this book for a more general search.
3. Click on the **Fetch It** button.

FactHound will fetch the best sites for you!

Read More

Kalman, Bobbie. *China: The Land.* The Lands, Peoples, and Cultures Series. New York: Crabtree, 2001.

Meister, Cari. *Yangtze River.* Rivers and Lakes. Edina, Minn.: Abdo, 2002.

Waterlow, Julia. *The Yangtze.* Great Rivers of the World. Milwaukee: World Almanac Library, 2003.

Index